and the
blessings
of the
Lord
rested upon us

Bible verses for every situation

Table of content:

What is this book about?

Often people search for inspiration, hope, and insight from family, friends, the workplace, or a number of other sources. Though others can offer words of encouragement, their words will fail to sustain our deepest needs. The Holy Scriptures provide God's words, ways, and will for our lives. He knows what is in our hearts, what dilemmas we are facing, and through His infinite love, He will guide us with perfection every time. The Scriptures are filled with comfort, solutions, and illustrations to face every situation in life.

In the tumultuous world we now live in, inspirational Bible verses give us definitive encouragement, provide hope, supply supernatural peace1 and an eternal promise. The greatest inspiration comes from knowing that God gave His Son, Jesus, to atone for our sins. His sacrifice on the cross is payment for our wrongs. When we accept it with sincerity and simple faith, we can inherit entry into the Kingdom of God.

The inspiration to become more righteous is found in numerous Scriptures. God is our Heavenly Father and wants us to succeed in the life He has planned for us. The Lord knows we have many needs, temptations, and that we face a diversity of difficult situations. Therefore, He provides His Holy Spirit as the Comforter who is available no matter how dire our circumstances

Healing Bible verses

The Bible speaks often of miraculous healing through the work of Jesus Christ and faith in God. Our Lord is able to provide comfort and healing for you and your loved ones.

This collection of Scriptures on healing will provide encouragement, strength, and comfort as you focus on God's healing power.

Praying Scripture back to God is a wonderful way to focus on his promises and provision. You can pray these Bible Verses out-loud over your life, sickness, and your loved ones.

It is evidenced through both Old Testament and New Testament Scripture that God does have the power to heal our physical bodies. Miraculous healings still happen today! Use these Bible verses to talk to God about your pain and to fill your heart with hope.

Scriptures About Physical Healing

- Heal me, O Lord, and I will be healed; save me and I will be saved, for you are the one I praise. - **Jeremiah 17:14**

- Is anyone among you sick? Let them call the elders of the church to pray over them and anoint them with oil in the name of the Lord. And the prayer offered in faith will make the sick person well; the Lord will raise them up. If they have sinned, they will be forgiven. - **James 5:14-15**

- "He said, "If you listen carefully to the LORD your God and do what is right in his eyes, if you pay attention to his commands and keep all his decrees, I will not bring on you any of the diseases I brought on the Egyptians, for I am the LORD, who heals you." - **Exodus 15:26**

- "Worship the LORD your God, and his blessing will be on your food and water. I will take away sickness from among you..." - **Exodus 23:25**

- "So do not fear, for I am with you; do not be dismayed, for I am your God. I will strengthen you and help you; I will uphold you with my righteous right hand." - **Isaiah 41:10**

- "Surely he took up our pain and bore our suffering, yet we considered him punished by God, stricken by him, and afflicted. But he was pierced for our transgressions, he was crushed for our iniquities; the punishment that brought us peace was on him, and by his wounds we are healed." - **Isaiah 53:4-5**

- "But I will restore you to health and heal your wounds,' declares the LORD" - **Jeremiah 30:17**

- "See now that I myself am he! There is no god besides me. I put to death and I bring to life, I have wounded and I will heal, and no one can deliver out of my hand." - **Deuteronomy 32:39**

- "if my people, who are called by my name, will humble themselves and pray and seek my face and turn from their wicked ways, then I will hear from heaven, and I will forgive their sin and will heal their land. Now my eyes will be open and my ears attentive to the prayers offered in this place." - **2 Chronicles 7:14-15**

- "You restored me to health and let me live. Surely it was for my benefit that I suffered such anguish. In your love you kept me from the pit of destruction; you have put all my sins behind your back." - **Isaiah 38:16-17**

- "I have seen their ways, but I will heal them; I will guide them and restore comfort to Israel's mourners, creating praise on their lips. Peace, peace, to those far and near," says the LORD. "And I will heal them." - **Isaiah 57:18-19**

- "Nevertheless, I will bring health and healing to it; I will heal my people and will let them enjoy abundant peace and security." - **Jeremiah 33:6**

- "Dear friend, I pray that you may enjoy good health and that all may go well with you, even as your soul is getting along well." - **3 John 1:2**

- "And my God will meet all your needs according to the riches of his glory in Christ Jesus." - **Philippians 4:19**

- "He will wipe every tear from their eyes. There will be no more death' or mourning or crying or pain, for the old order of things has passed away." - **Revelations 21:4**

Spiritual and Emotional Healing Scriptures

- "My son, pay attention to what I say; turn your ear to my words. Do not let them out of your sight, keep them within your heart; for they are life to those who find them and health to one's whole body." - **Proverbs 4:20-22**

- "A cheerful heart is good medicine, but a crushed spirit dries up the bones." - **Proverbs 17:22**

- "There is a time for everything, and a season for every activity under the heavens: a time to be born and a time to die, a time to plant and a time to uproot, a time to kill and a time to heal, a time to tear down and a time to build, a time to weep and a time to laugh, a time to mourn and a time to dance, a time to scatter stones and a time to gather them, a time to embrace and a time to refrain from embracing, a time to search and a time to give up, a time to keep and a time to throw away, a time to tear and a time to mend, a time to be silent and a time to speak, a time to love and a time to hate, a time for war and a time for peace." - **Ecclesiastes 3:1-8**

- "LORD, be gracious to us; we long for you. Be our strength every morning, our salvation in time of distress." - **Isaiah 33:2**

- "Therefore confess your sins to each other and pray for each other so that you may be healed. The prayer of a righteous person is powerful and effective." - **James 5:6**

- "He himself bore our sins" in his body on the cross, so that we might die to sins and live for righteousness; "by his wounds you have been healed." - **1 Peter 2:24**

- "Peace I leave with you; my peace I give you. I do not give to you as the world gives. Do not let your hearts be troubled and do not be afraid." - **John 14:27**

- "Come to me, all you who are weary and burdened, and I will give you rest. Take my yoke upon you and learn from me, for I am gentle and humble in heart, and you will find rest for your souls. For my yoke is easy and my burden is light." - **Matthew 11:28-30**

- "He gives strength to the weary and increases the power of the weak." - **Isaiah 40:2**

- "No temptation has overtaken you except what is common to mankind. And God is faithful; he will not let you be tempted beyond what you can bear. But when you are tempted, he will also provide a way out so that you can endure it." - **1 Corinthians 10:13**

Healing Verses from Psalms

- "Then they cried to the LORD in their trouble, and he saved them from their distress. He sent out his word and healed them; he rescued them from the grave. Let them give thanks to the LORD for his unfailing love and his wonderful deeds for mankind." - **Psalms 107:19-21**

- "LORD my God, I called to you for help, and you healed me." - **Psalms 30:2**

- "The righteous cry out, and the LORD hears them; he delivers them from all their troubles. The LORD is close to the brokenhearted and saves those who are crushed in spirit. The righteous person may have many troubles, but the LORD delivers him from them all; he protects all his bones, not one of them will be broken. Evil will slay the wicked; the foes of the righteous will be condemned. The LORD will rescue his servants; no one who takes refuge in him will be condemned." - **Psalms 34:17-22**

- "Praise the LORD, my soul, and forget not all his benefits - who forgives all your sins and heals all your diseases, who redeems your life from the pit and crowns you with love and compassion." - **Psalms 103:2-4**

- "Have mercy on me, LORD, for I am faint; heal me, LORD, for my bones are in agony." - **Psalms 6:2**

- "The LORD protects and preserves them— they are counted among the blessed in the land - he does not give them over to the desire of their foes. The LORD sustains them on their sickbed and restores them from their bed of illness." - **Psalms 41:2-3**

- "I said, "Have mercy on me, LORD; heal me, for I have sinned against you." - **Psalms 41:4**

- "He heals the brokenhearted and binds up their wounds." - **Psalms 147:3**

- "The LORD is my shepherd, I lack nothing. He makes me lie down in green pastures, he leads me beside quiet waters, he refreshes my soul. He guides me along the right paths for his name's sake. Even though I walk through the darkest valley,I will fear no evil, for you are with me; your rod and your staff, they comfort me. You prepare a table before me in the presence of my enemies. You anoint my head with oil; my cup overflows. Surely your goodness and love will follow me all the days of my life, and I will dwell in the house of the LORD forever." - **Psalms 23**

- "Hear, LORD, and be merciful to me; LORD, be my help." You turned my wailing into dancing; you removed my sackcloth and clothed me with joy" - **Psalms 30:10-11**

- "My flesh and my heart may fail, but God is the strength of my heart and my portion forever." - **Psalms 73:26**

Healing Miracles of Jesus

- "Jesus went throughout Galilee, teaching in their synagogues, proclaiming the good news of the kingdom, and healing every disease and sickness among the people. News about him spread all over Syria, and people brought to him all who were ill with various diseases, those suffering severe pain, the demon-possessed, those having seizures, and the paralyzed; and he healed them." - **Matthew 4:23-24**

- "Jesus called his twelve disciples to him and gave them authority to drive out impure spirits and to heal every disease and sickness...Heal the sick, raise the dead, cleanse those who have leprosy, drive out demons. Freely you have received; freely give." - **Matthew 10:1-8**

- "On hearing this, Jesus said to them, "It is not the healthy who need a doctor, but the sick. I have not come to call the righteous, but sinners." - **Mark 2:17**

- "Jesus went through all the towns and villages, teaching in their synagogues, proclaiming the good news of the kingdom and healing every disease and sickness." - **Matthew 9:35**

- "He said to her, "Daughter, your faith has healed you. Go in peace and be freed from your suffering." - **Mark 5:34**

- "One day Jesus was teaching, and Pharisees and teachers of the law were sitting there. They had come from every village of Galilee and from Judea and Jerusalem. And the power of the Lord was with Jesus to heal the sick. Some men came carrying a paralyzed man on a mat and tried to take him into the house to lay him before Jesus. When they could not find a way to do this because of the crowd, they went up on the roof and lowered him on his mat through the tiles into the middle of the crowd, right in front of Jesus. When Jesus saw their faith, he said, "Friend, your sins are forgiven." The Pharisees and the teachers of the law began thinking to themselves, "Who is this fellow who speaks blasphemy? Who can forgive sins but God alone?" Jesus knew what they were thinking and asked, "Why are you thinking these things in your hearts? Which is easier: to say, 'Your sins are forgiven,' or to say, 'Get up and walk'? But I want you to know that the Son of Man has authority on earth to forgive sins." So he said to the paralyzed man, "I tell you, get up, take your mat and go home." Immediately he stood up in front of them, took what he had been lying on and went home praising God. Everyone was amazed and gave praise to God. They were filled with awe and said, "We have seen remarkable things today." - **Luke 5:17-24**

- "And a woman was there who had been crippled by a spirit for eighteen years. She was bent over and could not straighten up at all. When Jesus saw her, he called her forward and said to her, "Woman, you are set free from your infirmity." Then he put his hands on her, and immediately she straightened up and praised God." - **Luke 13:11-13**

- "One Sabbath, when Jesus went to eat in the house of a prominent Pharisee, he was being carefully watched. There in front of him was a man suffering from abnormal swelling of his body. Jesus asked the Pharisees and experts in the law, "Is it lawful to heal on the Sabbath or not?" But they remained silent. So taking hold of the man, he healed him and sent him on his way. Then he asked them, "If one of you has a childor an ox that falls into a well on the Sabbath day, will you not immediately pull it out?" And they had nothing to say." - **Luke 14:1-6**

- "Stretch out your hand to heal and perform signs and wonders through the name of your holy servant Jesus." After they prayed, the place where they were meeting was shaken. And they were all filled with the Holy Spirit and spoke the word of God boldly." - **Acts 4:30-31**

- "There he found a man named Aeneas, who was paralyzed and had been bedridden for eight years. "Aeneas," Peter said to him, "Jesus Christ heals you. Get up and roll up your mat." Immediately Aeneas got up." - **Acts 9:33-34**

- "You know what has happened throughout the province of Judea, beginning in Galilee after the baptism that John preached - how God anointed Jesus of Nazareth with the Holy Spirit and power, and how he went around doing good and healing all who were under the power of the devil, because God was with him." - **Acts 10:37-38**

- "As he was going into a village, ten men who had leprosy met him. They stood at a distance and called out in a loud voice, "Jesus, Master, have pity on us!" When he saw them, he said, "Go, show yourselves to the priests." And as they went, they were cleansed. One of them, when he saw he was healed, came back, praising God in a loud voice. He threw himself at Jesus' feet and thanked him—and he was a Samaritan. Jesus asked, "Were not all ten cleansed? Where are the other nine? Has no one returned to give praise to God except this foreigner?" Then he said to him, "Rise and go; your faith has made you well." - **Luke 12:17-19**

- "While I am in the world, I am the light of the world." After saying this, he spit on the ground, made some mud with the saliva, and put it on the man's eyes. "Go," he told him, "wash in the Pool of Siloam" (this word means "Sent"). So the man went and washed, and came home seeing. His neighbors and those who had formerly seen him begging asked, "Isn't this the same man who used to sit and beg?" Some claimed that he was. Others said, "No, he only looks like him." But he himself insisted, "I am the man." "How then were your eyes opened?" they asked. He replied, "The man they call Jesus made some mud and put it on my eyes. He told me to go to Siloam and wash. So I went and washed, and then I could see." - **John 9:5-11**

- "As soon as they left the synagogue, they went with James and John to the home of Simon and Andrew. Simon's mother-in-law was in bed with a fever, and they immediately told Jesus about her. So he went to her, took her hand and helped her up. The fever left her and she began to wait on them. That evening after sunset the people brought to Jesus all the sick and demon-possessed. The whole town gathered at the door, and Jesus healed many who had various diseases. He also drove out many demons, but he would not let the demons speak because they knew who he was." - **Mark 1:29-34**

- "While Jesus was still speaking, someone came from the house of Jairus, the synagogue leader. "Your daughter is dead," he said. "Don't bother the teacher anymore." Hearing this, Jesus said to Jairus, "Don't be afraid; just believe, and she will be healed." When he arrived at the house of Jairus, he did not let anyone go in with him except Peter, John and James, and the child's father and mother. Meanwhile, all the people were wailing and mourning for her. "Stop wailing," Jesus said. "She is not dead but asleep." They laughed at him, knowing that she was dead. But he took her by the hand and said, "My child, get up!" Her spirit returned, and at once she stood up. Then Jesus told them to give her something to eat. Her parents were astonished, but he ordered them not to tell anyone what had happened." - **Luke 8:49-56**

Bible Verses of Strength

- "My flesh and my heart may fail, but God is the strength of my heart and my portion forever." - **Psalm 73:26**

- "Then they cried to the Lord in their trouble, and he saved them from their distress. He sent forth his word and healed them, he rescued them from the grave." - **Psalm 107:19-20**

- "Heal me, O Lord, and I shall be healed; save me, and I shall be saved, for you are my praise." - **Jeremiah 17:14**

- "'Not by might nor by power, but by my Spirit,' says the LORD Almighty." - **Zechariah 4:6**

- "God is our refuge and strength, an ever-present help in trouble." - **Psalm 46:1**

- "Come to me, all you who are weary and burdened, and I will give you rest." - **Matthew 11:28**

- "The LORD replied, "My Presence will go with you, and I will give you rest." - **Exodus 33:14**

- "The LORD will fight for you; you need only to be still." Exodus - **14:14**

- But He said to me, "My grace is sufficient for you, for My power is perfected in weakness." Therefore I will boast all the more gladly in my weaknesses, so that the power of Christ may rest on me. That is why, for the sake of Christ, I delight in weaknesses, in insults, in hardships, in persecutions, in difficulties. For when I am weak, then I am strong." - **2 Corinthians 12:9-10**

- "Do not be anxious about anything, but in every situation, by prayer and petition, with thanksgiving, present your requests to God. And the peace of God, which transcends all understanding, will guard your hearts and your minds in Christ Jesus." - **Philippians 4:6-7**

- "Put on the full armor of God, so that you will be able to stand firm against the schemes of the devil. For our struggle is not against flesh and blood, but against the rulers, against the powers, against the world forces of this darkness, against the spiritual forces of wickedness in the heavenly places. Therefore, take up the full armor of God, so that you will be able to resist in the evil day, and having done everything, to stand firm." - **Ephesians 6:11-13**

- "...by His wounds we are healed." - **Isaiah 53:5**

- "But those who hope in the LORD will renew their strength. They will soar on wings like eagles; they will run and not grow weary, they will walk and not be faint." - **Isaiah 40:31**

- "...Do not be grieved, for the joy of the LORD is your strength." - **Nehemiah 8:10**

- "But he knows the way that I take; when he has tested me, I will come forth as gold." - **Job 23:10**

Psalms for People Who Struggle with Anxiety

- "God, You are my shepherd, I lack nothing. You make me lie down in green pastures, You lead me beside still waters, You restore my soul. You lead me in paths of righteousness for Your name's sake. Even though I walk through the valley of the shadow of death, I will fear no evil, for you are with me! Your rod and your staff, they comfort me! You prepare a table before me in the presence of my enemies, You anoint my head with oil, my cup overflows. Surely goodness and mercy will follow me all the days of my life and I will dwell in Your house forever. Amen." - **Psalm 23:1-6**

- "God, You are my light and my salvation, whom shall I fear? You are the strength of my life, of whom shall I be afraid? When the wicked come against me to eat up my flesh, my enemies and foes, they stumbled and fell. Though an army may encamp against me, my heart shall not fear!" - **Psalm 27:1-3**

- "I will bless You at all times, Your praise will continually be in my mouth. I sought You, Lord, and You heard me, You delivered me from all my fears. When we look to You we are radiant. Your angels encamp all around those who fear You and You deliver us. Help me to taste and see that You are good, oh Lord. You say I will be blessed when I trust You. Those who seek You lack no good thing." - **Psalm 34:1-10**

- "Hear my cry, O God; from the ends of the earth I cry to You, when my heart is overwhelmed, lead me to the rock that is higher than I. For you are a shelter for me, a strong tower from the enemy..." - **Psalm 61:1-3**

- "You are my refuge and my fortress, my God, in whom I trust." - **Psalm 91:2**

- "Do not be anxious about anything, but in every situation, by prayer and petition, with thanksgiving, present your requests to God. And the peace of God, which transcends all understanding, will guard your hearts and your minds in Christ Jesus." - **Philippians 4:4-6**

Inspirational Bible Verses

Inspiration is subjective, as different people will find different things to be inspiring. However, Christians can unite around one inspirational source— God himself. God is the basis for all of our inspiration because He is the basis for everything good and everything worth imitating.

- "Judge not, and ye shall not be judged; condemn not, and ye shall not be condemned; forgive, and ye shall be forgiven." - **Luke 6:37**

- "And Jesus said unto them... "If ye have faith as a grain of mustard seed, ye shall say unto this mountain, remove hence to yonder place; and it shall remove; and nothing shall be impossible to you." - **Matthew 17:20**

- "It is God who arms me with strength and makes my way perfect. He makes my feet like the feet of a deer; he enables me to stand on the heights. He trains my hands for battle; my arms can bend a bow of bronze. You give me your shield of victory, and your right hand sustains me; you stoop down to make me great. You broaden the path beneath me, so that my ankles do not turn." - **Psalm 18:32-36**

- "So do not fear, for I am with you; do not be dismayed, for I am your God. I will strengthen you and help you; I will uphold you with my righteous right hand." - **Isaiah 41:10**

- "Be strong and courageous. Do not be afraid or terrified because of them, for the Lord your God goes with you; he will never leave you nor forsake you." - **Deuteronomy 31:6**

- "There is neither Jew nor Greek, there is neither bond nor free, there is neither male nor female: for ye are all one in Christ." - **Galatians 3:28**

- "But the fruit of the Spirit is love, joy, peace, patience, kindness, goodness, faithfulness, gentleness, self control. Against such there is no law. And those who are Christ's have crucified the flesh with its passions and desires. If we all live in the Spirit, let us also walk in the Spirit. Let us not become conceited, provoking one another, envying one another." - **Galatians 5:22-26**

- "The Lord is my light and my salvation - whom shall I fear? The Lord is the stronghold of my life - of whom shall I be afraid?" - **Psalm 27:1**

- "Beloved, let us love one another, for love is from God, and whoever loves has been born of God and knows God. Anyone who does not love does not know God, because God is love." - **1 John 4:7-8**

- "Do not let your hearts be troubled. Trust in God; trust also in me. In my Father's house are many rooms; if it were not so, I would have told you. I am going there to prepare a place for you. And if I go and prepare a place for you, I will come back and take you to be with me that you also may be where I am." - **John 14:1-3**

- "The Lord is my shepherd; I shall not want. He maketh me to lie down in green pastures: he leadeth me beside the still waters. He restoreth my soul: he leadeth me in the paths of righteousness for his name's sake. Even though I walk through the valley of the shadow of death, I will fear no evil, for you are with me; your rod and your staff, they comfort me. Thou preparest a table before me in the presence of mine enemies: thou anointest my head with oil; my cup runneth over. Surely goodness and mercy shall follow me all the days of my life: and I will dwell in the house of the Lord forever." - **Psalm 23**

- "And be ye kind one to another, tender-hearted, forgiving one another, even as God for Christ's sake hath forgiven you." - **Ephesians 4:32**

- "Lord, you have assigned me my portion and my cup; you have made my lot secure. The boundary lines have fallen for me in pleasant places; surely I have a delightful inheritance. I will praise the Lord, who counsels me; even at night my heart instructs me. I have set the Lord always before me. Because he is at my right hand, I will not be shaken." - **Psalm 16:5-8**

- "So we do not lose heart. Though our outer self is wasting away, our inner self is being renewed day by day. For this light momentary affliction is preparing for us an eternal weight of glory beyond all comparison, as we look not to the things that are seen but to the things that are unseen. For the things that are seen are transient, but the things that are unseen are eternal." - **Corinthians 4:16-18**

- "Even though I walk through the valley of the shadow of death, I will fear no evil, for you are with me; your rod and your staff, they comfort me." - **Psalm 23:4**

Motivational Bible Verses

The Bible is one of the best books for motivation that one can turn to any-time, be it in harrowing times or in times of happiness. Though written by human hands, the Holy Bible is believed to be the word of God. It is said to be inspired by the Holy Spirit, and when you read any Bible verse, you will feel peaceful from the depth of your heart. The Bible is replete with motivational verses, and from time immemorial, people have gained wisdom, reasons to get motivated, and also to motivate others by reading verses from this book.

- "The Lord is my shepherd; I shall not want. He maketh me to lie down in green pastures: he leadeth me beside the still waters. He restoreth my soul: he leadeth me in the paths of righteousness for his name's sake. Yea, though I walk through the valley of the shadow of death, I will fear no evil: for thou art with me; thy rod and thy staff they comfort me. Thou preparest a table before me in the presence of mine enemies: thou anointest my head with oil; my cup runneth over. Surely goodness and mercy shall follow me all the days of my life: and I will dwell in the house of the Lord forever." - Psalm 23

- The steps of a man are established by the LORD; And He delights in his way. When he falls, he shall not be hurled headlong; Because the LORD is the One who holds his hand. - **Psalm 37:23-24**

- Let your character be free from the love of money, being content with what you have; for He Himself has said, "I will never desert you, nor will I ever forsake you. - **Hebrews 13:5**

- I can do all things through Him who strengthens me. - **Philippians 4:13**

- Yet those who wait for the LORD Will gain new strength; They will mount up with wings like eagles, They will run and not get tired, They will walk and not become weary. - **Isaiah 40:31**

- Trust in the LORD, and do good; so shalt thou dwell in the land, and verily thou shalt be fed. Delight thyself also in the LORD: and he shall give thee the desires of thine heart. Commit thy way unto the LORD; trust also in him; and he shall bring it to pass. - **Psalm 37:3-5**

- Reflect on what I am saying, for the Lord will give you insight into all this. - **2 Timothy 2:5-7**

- Do not be anxious about anything, but in everything, by prayer and petition, with thanksgiving, present your requests to God. - **Philippians 4:6**

- Let your character be free from the love of money, being content with what you have; for He Himself has said, "I will never desert you, nor will I ever forsake you. - **Hebrews 13:5**

- Yet those who wait for the LORD Will gain new strength; They will mount up with wings like eagles, They will run and not get tired, They will walk and not become weary. - **Isaiah 40:31**

- Trust in the LORD, and do good; so shalt thou dwell in the land, and verily thou shalt be fed. Delight thyself also in the LORD: and he shall give thee the desires of thine heart. Commit thy way unto the LORD; trust also in him; and he shall bring it to pass. - **Psalm 37:3-5**

- Do not be anxious about anything, but in everything, by prayer and petition, with thanksgiving, present your requests to God. - **Philippians 4:6**

- If you can believe, all things are possible to him who believeth. - **Mark 9:23**

- Cast your burden on the LORD, And He shall sustain you; He shall never permit the righteous to be moved. - **Psalm 55:22**

- But certainly God has heard me; He has attended to the voice of my prayer. Blessed be God, Who has not turned away my prayer, Nor His mercy from me! - **Psalm 66:19-20**

- For I know the plans I have for you," declares the LORD, "plans to prosper you and not to harm you, plans to give you hope and a future. Then you will call upon me and come and pray to me, and I will listen to you. You will seek me and find me when you seek me with all your heart. I will be found by you," declares the LORD, "and will bring you back from captivity. I will gather you from all the nations and places where I have banished you," declares the LORD, "and will bring you back to the place from which I carried you into exile. - **Jeremiah 29:11-14**

- Don't let anyone look down on you because you are young, but set an example for the believers in speech, in life, in love, in faith and in purity. - **1 Timothy 4:12**

- Listen, my son, to your father's instruction and do not forsake your mother's teaching. They will be a garland to grace your head and a chain to adorn your neck. - **Proverbs 1:8-9**

- Do not let your hearts be troubled. Trust in God; trust also in me. - **John 14:1**

- Fear thou not... I will strengthen thee... I will help thee. - **Isaiah 41:10**

- For God so loved the world that he gave his one and only Son, that whoever believes in him shall not perish but have eternal life. - **John 3:16**

- Young men, in the same way be submissive to those who are older. All of you, clothe yourselves with humility toward one another, because, "God opposes the proud but gives grace to the humble." Humble yourselves, therefore, under God's mighty hand, that he may lift you up in due time. Cast all your anxiety on him because he cares for you. Be self-controlled and alert. Your enemy the devil prowls around like a roaring lion looking for someone to devour. Resist him, standing firm in the faith, because you know that your brothers throughout the world are undergoing the same kind of sufferings. **- 1 Peter 5:5-9**

- Remember your Creator in the days of your youth, before the days of trouble come and the years approach when you will say, "I find no pleasure in them". **- Ecclesiastes 12:1**

- My soul, wait silently for God alone, For my expectation is from Him. He only is my rock and my salvation; He is my defense; I shall not be moved. In God is my salvation and my glory; The rock of my strength, And my refuge, is in God. Trust in Him at all times, you people; Pour out your heart before Him; God is a refuge for us. **- Psalm 62:5-8**

- In the Lord, put your trust. **- Psalms 11:1**

- And he said, "The LORD is my rock and my fortress and my deliverer; My God, my rock, in whom I take refuge; My shield and the horn of my salvation, my stronghold and my refuge; My savior, Thou dost save me from violence. "I call upon the LORD, who is worthy to be praised; And I am saved from my enemies **- 2 Samuel 22:2-4**

- These things I have spoken to you, that in Me you may have peace. In the world you have tribulation, but take courage; I have overcome the world. **- John 16:33**

- How blessed is he who considers the helpless; The LORD will deliver him in a day of trouble. The LORD will protect him, and keep him alive, And he shall be called blessed upon the earth; And do not give him over to the desire of his enemies. The LORD will sustain him upon his sickbed; In his illness, Thou dost restore him to health. - **Psalm 41:1-3**

- Therefore, take up the full armor of God, that you may be able to resist in the evil day, and having done everything, to stand firm. - **Ephesians 6:13**

- Though I walk in the midst of trouble, Thou wilt revive me; Thou wilt stretch forth Thy hand against the wrath of my enemies, And Thy right hand will save me. - **Psalm 138:7**

- Trust in the LORD with all your heart, And do not lean on your own understanding. In all your ways acknowledge Him, And He will make your paths straight - **Proverbs 3:5-6**

- I will not be afraid of ten thousands of the people That have set themselves against me round about. - **Psalm 3:6**

- The LORD also will be a stronghold for the oppressed, A stronghold in times of trouble. - **Psalm 9:9**

- The LORD is the one who goes ahead of you; He will be with you. He will not fail you or forsake you. Do not fear or be dismayed. - **Deuteronomy 31:8**

- And the light shines in the darkness, and the darkness did not comprehend it. - **John 1:5**

Bible Verses for the Broken-hearted

- My flesh and my heart may fail, but God is the strength of my heart and my portion forever. - **Psalms 73:26**

- Fear not, for I am with you; be not dismayed, for I am your God; I will strengthen you, I will help you, I will uphold you with my righteous right hand. - **Isaiah 41:10**

- Come to me, all who labor and are heavy laden, and I will give you rest. Take my yoke upon you, and learn from me, for I am gentle and lowly in heart, and you will find rest for your souls. For my yoke is easy, and my burden is light." - **Matthew 11:28-30**

- Peace I leave with you; my peace I give to you. Not as the world gives do I give to you. Let not your hearts be troubled, neither let them be afraid. - **John 14:27**

- But he said to me, "My grace is sufficient for you, for my power is made perfect in weakness." Therefore I will boast all the more gladly of my weaknesses, so that the power of Christ may rest upon me. - **2 Corinthians 12:9**

- Cast your burden on the LORD, and he will sustain you; he will never permit the righteous to be moved. - **Psalms 55:22**

- He sent out his word and healed them, and delivered them from their destruction. - **Psalms 107:20**

- He heals the brokenhearted and binds up their wounds. - **Psalms 147:3**

- Trust in the LORD with all your heart, and do not lean on your own understanding. In all your ways acknowledge him, and he will make straight your paths. - **Proverbs 3:5-6**

- He himself bore our sins in his body on the tree, that we might die to sin and live to righteousness. By his wounds you have been healed. - **1 Peter 2:24**

- Therefore let those who suffer according to God's will entrust their souls to a faithful Creator while doing good. - **1 Peter 4:19**

- Remember not the former things, nor consider the things of old. - **Isaiah 43:18**

- Truly, I say to you, whoever says to this mountain, 'Be taken up and thrown into the sea,' and does not doubt in his heart, but believes that what he says will come to pass, it will be done for him. - **Mark 11:23**

- Therefore, since we have been justified by faith, we have peace with God through our Lord Jesus Christ. Through him we have also obtained access by faith into this grace in which we stand, and we rejoice in hope of the glory of God. - **Romans 5:1-2**

- And we know that for those who love God all things work together for good, for those who are called according to his purpose. - **Romans 8:28**

- Love bears all things, believes all things, hopes all things, endures all things. - **1 Corinthians 13:7**

- So we are always of good courage. We know that while we are at home in the body we are away from the Lord, for we walk by faith, not by sight. - **2 Corinthians 5:6-7**

- Brothers, I do not consider that I have made it my own. But one thing I do: forgetting what lies behind and straining forward to what lies ahead, I press on toward the goal for the prize of the upward call of God in Christ Jesus. - **Philippians 3:13-14**

- And I heard a loud voice from the throne saying, "Behold, the dwelling place of God is with man. He will dwell with them, and they will be his people, and God himself will be with them as their God. He will wipe away every tear from their eyes, and death shall be no more, neither shall there be mourning, nor crying, nor pain anymore, for the former things have passed away." - **Revelation 21:3-4**

Hope and Faith Bible Verse

The greatest hope in the Christian faith is that of eternal life. This hope is based on Jesus Christ and your relationship with Him. Write down one of these verses to reflect on in times of need.

- For the evil man has no future; the lamp of the wicked will be put out. **- Proverbs 24:20**

- Know that wisdom is such to your soul; if you find it, there will be a future, and your hope will not be cut off. **- Proverbs 24:14**

- For I know the plans I have for you, declares the LORD, plans for welfare and not for evil, to give you a future and a hope. **- Jeremiah 29:11**

- Paul, a servant of God and an apostle of Jesus Christ, for the sake of the faith of God's elect and their knowledge of the truth, which accords with godliness, in hope of eternal life, which God, who never lies, promised before the ages began **- Titus 1:1-2**

- So that being justified by his grace we might become heirs according to the hope of eternal life. **- Titus 3:7**

- If in Christ we have hope in this life only, we are of all people most to be pitied. **- 1 Corinthians 15:19**

- So we do not lose heart. Though our outer self is wasting away, our inner self is being renewed day by day. For this light momentary affliction is preparing for us an eternal weight of glory beyond all comparison, as we look not to the things that are seen but to the things that are unseen. For the things that are seen are transient, but the things that are unseen are eternal. - 2 **Corinthians 4:16-18**

- Blessed be the God and Father of our Lord Jesus Christ! According to his great mercy, he has caused us to be born again to a living hope through the resurrection of Jesus Christ from the dead - **1 Peter 1:3**

- Through him we have also obtained access by faith into this grace in which we stand, and we rejoice in hope of the glory of God. More than that, we rejoice in our sufferings, knowing that suffering produces endurance, and endurance produces character, and character produces hope, and hope does not put us to shame, because God's love has been poured into our hearts through the Holy Spirit who has been given to us. - **Romans 5:2-5**

- For in this hope we were saved. Now hope that is seen is not hope. For who hopes for what he sees? But if we hope for what we do not see, we wait for it with patience. - **Romans 8:24-25**

- Rejoice in hope, be patient in tribulation, be constant in prayer. - **Romans 12:12**

- For whatever was written in former days was written for our instruction, that through endurance and through the encouragement of the Scriptures we might have hope. - **Romans 15:4**

- May the God of hope fill you with all joy and peace in believing, so that by the power of the Holy Spirit you may abound in hope. - **Romans 15:13**

- One thing have I asked of the LORD, that will I seek after: that I may dwell in the house of the LORD all the days of my life, to gaze upon the beauty of the LORD and to inquire in his temple. For he will hide me in his shelter in the day of trouble; he will conceal me under the cover of his tent; he will lift me high upon a rock. - **Psalm 27:4-5**

- While he was still speaking, there came from the ruler's house some who said, "Your daughter is dead. Why trouble the Teacher any further?" But overhearing what they said, Jesus said to the ruler of the synagogue, "Do not fear, only believe." - **Mark 5:35-36**

- The LORD your God is in your midst, a mighty one who will save; he will rejoice over you with gladness; he will quiet you by his love; he will exult over you with loud singing. - **Zephaniah 3:17**

- Jesus said to her, "Everyone who drinks of this water will be thirsty again, but whoever drinks of the water that I will give him will never be thirsty again. The water that I will give him will become in him a spring of water welling up to eternal life." - **John 4:13-14**

- Now faith is the assurance of things hoped for, the conviction of things not seen. - **Hebrews 11:1**

- Seek the LORD and his strength; seek his presence continually! - **1 Chronicles 16:11**

- No temptation has overtaken you that is not common to man. God is faithful, and he will not let you be tempted beyond your ability, but with the temptation he will also provide the way of escape, that you may be able to endure it. - **1 Corinthians 10:13**

- Since we have the same spirit of faith according to what has been written, "I believed, and so I spoke," we also believe, and so we also speak, knowing that he who raised the Lord Jesus will raise us also with Jesus and bring us with you into his presence. - **2 Corinthians 4:13-14**

- Be watchful, stand firm in the faith, act like men, be strong. - **1 Corinthians 16:13**

- And Jesus said to him, "Go your way; your faith has made you well." And immediately he recovered his sight and followed him on the way. - **Mark 10:52**

- Trust in the LORD with all your heart, and do not lean on your own understanding. - **Proverbs 3:5**

- "Be still, and know that I am God. I will be exalted among the nations, I will be exalted in the earth!" - **Psalm 46:10**

- And without faith it is impossible to please him, for whoever would draw near to God must believe that he exists and that he rewards those who seek him. - **Hebrews 11:6**

- "Hear, O Israel: The LORD our God, the LORD is one. You shall love the LORD your God with all your heart and with all your soul and with all your might. - **Deuteronomy 6:4-5**
- This is the day that the LORD has made; let us rejoice and be glad in it. - **Psalm 118:24**

Bible Verses About Love

The Bible is full of great verses and passages about the topic of love. God's love for us is a perfect example and starting place to study on love. There are also great verses about love in relation to marriage, brotherly love or friendship, and loving your neighbor.

- Love is patient and kind; love does not envy or boast; it is not arrogant or rude. It does not insist on its own way; it is not irritable or resentful; it does not rejoice at wrongdoing, but rejoices with the truth. Love bears all things, believes all things, hopes all things, endures all things. Love never ends. As for prophecies, they will pass away; as for tongues, they will cease; as for knowledge, it will pass away. - **1 Corinthians 13:4-8**

- "For God so loved the world, that he gave his only Son, that whoever believes in him should not perish but have eternal life. - **John 3:16**

- But God shows his love for us in that while we were still sinners, Christ died for us. - **Romans 5:8**

- Galatians 2:20 I have been crucified with Christ. It is no longer I who live, but Christ who lives in me. And the life I now live in the flesh I live by faith in the Son of God, who loved me and gave himself for me. - **Romans 8:37-39**

- See what kind of love the Father has given to us, that we should be called children of God; and so we are. The reason why the world does not know us is that it did not know him. - **1 John 3:1**

- Owe no one anything, except to love each other, for the one who loves another has fulfilled the law. - **Romans 13:8**

- For you were called to freedom, brothers. Only do not use your freedom as an opportunity for the flesh, but through love serve one another. - **Galatians 5:13**

- With all humility and gentleness, with patience, bearing with one another in love - **Ephesians 4:2**

- Having purified your souls by your obedience to the truth for a sincere brotherly love, love one another earnestly from a pure heart - **1 Peter 1:22**

- Beloved, let us love one another, for love is from God, and whoever loves has been born of God and knows God. - **1 John 4:7**

- "You have heard that it was said, 'You shall love your neighbor and hate your enemy.' But I say to you, Love your enemies and pray for those who persecute you, so that you may be sons of your Father who is in heaven. For he makes his sun rise on the evil and on the good, and sends rain on the just and on the unjust. For if you love those who love you, what reward do you have? Do not even the tax collectors do the same? And if you greet only your brothers, what more are you doing than others? Do not even the Gentiles do the same? You therefore must be perfect, as your heavenly Father is perfect. - **Matthew 5:43-48**

- "No one can serve two masters, for either he will hate the one and love the other, or he will be devoted to the one and despise the other. You cannot serve God and money. "Therefore I tell you, do not be anxious about your life, what you will eat or what you will drink, nor about your body, what you will put on. Is not life more than food, and the body more than clothing? - **Matthew 6:24-25**

- And one of the scribes came up and heard them disputing with one another, and seeing that he answered them well, asked him, "Which commandment is the most important of all?" Jesus answered, "The most important is, 'Hear, O Israel: The Lord our God, the Lord is one. And you shall love the Lord your God with all your heart and with all your soul and with all your mind and with all your strength.' - **Mark 12:28-30**

- Whoever has my commandments and keeps them, he it is who loves me. And he who loves me will be loved by my Father, and I will love him and manifest myself to him." Judas (not Iscariot) said to him, "Lord, how is it that you will manifest yourself to us, and not to the world?" Jesus answered him, "If anyone loves me, he will keep my word, and my Father will love him, and we will come to him and make our home with him. Whoever does not love me does not keep my words. And the word that you hear is not mine but the Father's who sent me. - **John 14:21-24**

- As the Father has loved me, so have I loved you. Abide in my love. If you keep my commandments, you will abide in my love, just as I have kept my Father's commandments and abide in his love. These things I have spoken to you, that my joy may be in you, and that your joy may be full. "This is my commandment, that you love one another as I have loved you. Greater love has no one than this, that someone lay down his life for his friends. You are my friends if you do what I command you. No longer do I call you servants, for the servant does not know what his master is doing; but I have called you friends, for all that I have heard from my Father I have made known to you. You did not choose me, but I chose you and appointed you that you should go and bear fruit and that your fruit should abide, so that whatever you ask the Father in my name, he may give it to you. These things I command you, so that you will love one another. - **John 15:9-17**

- Set me as a seal upon your heart, as a seal upon your arm, for love is strong as death, jealousy is fierce as the grave. Its flashes are flashes of fire, the very flame of the LORD. Many waters cannot quench love, neither can floods drown it. If a man offered for love all the wealth of his house, he would be utterly despised. - **Song of Solomon 8:6-7**

- With all humility and gentleness, with patience, bearing with one another in love, eager to maintain the unity of the Spirit in the bond of peace. - **Ephesians 4:2-3**

- Complete my joy by being of the same mind, having the same love, being in full accord and of one mind. - **Philippians 2:2**

- Little children, let us not love in word or talk but in deed and in truth. - **1 John 3:18**

- You prepare a table before me in the presence of my enemies; you anoint my head with oil; my cup overflows. Surely goodness and mercy shall follow me all the days of my life, and I shall dwell in the house of the LORD forever. - **Psalm 23:5-6**

- Make your face shine on your servant; save me in your steadfast love! - **Psalm 31:16**

- Because your steadfast love is better than life, my lips will praise you. - **Psalm 63:3**

- Hatred stirs up strife, but love covers all offenses. - **Proverbs 10:12**

Bible Verses About Worry

- "Therefore I tell you, do not be anxious about your life, what you will eat or what you will drink, nor about your body, what you will put on. Is not life more than food, and the body more than clothing? Look at the birds of the air: they neither sow nor reap nor gather into barns, and yet your heavenly Father feeds them. Are you not of more value than they? And which of you by being anxious can add a single hour to his span of life? - **Matthew 6:25-27**

- "Therefore do not be anxious about tomorrow, for tomorrow will be anxious for itself. Sufficient for the day is its own trouble. - **Matthew 6:34**

- Come to me, all who labor and are heavy laden, and I will give you rest. Take my yoke upon you, and learn from me, for I am gentle and lowly in heart, and you will find rest for your souls. For my yoke is easy, and my burden is light." - **Matthew 11:28-30**

- And which of you by being anxious can add a single hour to his span of life? - **Luke 12:25**

- Peace I leave with you;my peace I give to you. Not as the world gives do I give to you. Let not your hearts be troubled, neither let them be afraid. - **John 14:27**

- And let the peace of Christ rule in your hearts, to which indeed you were called in one body. And be thankful. - **Colossians 3:15**

- Now may the Lord of peace himself give you peace at all times in every way. The Lord be with you all. - **2 Thessalonians 3:16**

- Cast your burden on the LORD, and he will sustain you; he will never permit the righteous to be moved. - **Psalm 55:22**

- Anxiety in a man's heart weighs him down, but a good word makes him glad. - **Proverbs 12:25**

- Do not be anxious about anything, but in everything by prayer and supplication with thanksgiving let your requests be made known to God. And the peace of God, which surpasses all understanding, will guard your hearts and your minds in Christ Jesus. - **Philippians 4:6-7**

- Casting all your anxieties on him, because he cares for you. - **1 Peter 5:7**

- Even though I walk through the valley of the shadow of death, I will fear no evil, for You are with me; your rod and your staff, they comfort me. - **Psalm 23:4**

- But now thus says the LORD, he who created you, O Jacob, he who formed you, O Israel: "Fear not, for I have redeemed you; I have called you by name, you are mine. When you pass through the waters, I will be with you; and through the rivers, they shall not overwhelm you; when you walk through fire you shall not be burned, and the flame shall not consume you. For I am the LORD your God, the Holy One of Israel, your Savior. I give Egypt as your ransom, Cush and Seba in exchange for you. - **Isaiah 43:1-3**

- So we can confidently say, "The Lord is my helper; I will not fear; what can man do to me?" - **Hebrews 13:6**

- "Be still, and know that I am God. I will be exalted among the nations; I will be exalted in the earth!" - **Psalm 46:10**

- When I am afraid, I put my trust in you. - **Psalm 56:3**

- I lift up my eyes to the hills. From where does my help come? My help comes from the LORD, who made heaven and earth. - **Psalm 121:1-2**

- Trust in the LORD with all your heart, and do not lean on your own understanding. In all your ways acknowledge him, and he will make straight your paths. - **Proverbs 3:5-6**

- No temptation has overtaken you that is not common to man. God is faithful, and he will not let you be tempted beyond your ability, but with the temptation he will also provide the way of escape, that you may be able to endure it. **- 1 Corinthians 10:13**

- What then shall we say to these things? If God is for us, who can be against us? **- Romans 8:31**

Bible Verses About God's Timing

- "For still the vision awaits its appointed time; it hastens to the end—it will not lie. If it seems slow, wait for it; it will surely come; it will not delay." - **Habakkuk 2:3**

- "But when the fullness of time had come, God sent forth his Son, born of woman, born under the law, to redeem those who were under the law, so that we might receive adoption as sons." - **Galatians 4:4-5**

- "For while we were still weak, at the right time Christ died for the ungodly." - **Romans 5:6**

- "Wait for the Lord; be strong, and let your heart take courage; wait for the Lord!" - **Psalm 27:14**

- "But they who wait for the Lord shall renew their strength; they shall mount up with wings like eagles; they shall run and not be weary; they shall walk and not faint." - **Isaiah 40:31**

- "He has made everything beautiful in its time. Also, he has put eternity into man's heart, yet so that he cannot find out what God has done from the beginning to the end." - **Ecclesiastes 3:11**

- "Lest you be wise in your own sight, I do not want you to be unaware of this mystery, brothers: a partial hardening has come upon Israel, until the fullness of the Gentiles has come in." - **Romans 11:25**

- "Is anything too hard for the Lord? At the appointed time I will return to you, about this time next year, and Sarah shall have a son." - **Genesis 18:14**

Bible Verses For Stress

- Peace I leave with you; my peace I give to you. Not as the world gives do I give to you. Let not your hearts be troubled, neither let them be afraid. - **John 14:27**

- Even youths shall faint and be weary, and young men shall fall exhausted; but they who wait for the LORD shall renew their strength; they shall mount up with wings like eagles; they shall run and not be weary; they shall walk and not faint. - **Isaiah 40:30, 31**

- But for you who fear my name, the sun of righteousness shall rise with healing in its wings. You shall go out leaping like calves from the stall. - **Malachi 4:2**

- For to set the mind on the flesh is death, but to set the mind on the Spirit is life and peace. - **Romans 8:6**

- The God of peace will soon crush Satan under your feet. The grace of our Lord Jesus Christ be with you. - **Romans 16:20**

- Do not be anxious about anything, but in everything by prayer and supplication with thanksgiving let your requests be made known to God. And the peace of God, which surpasses all understanding, will guard your hearts and your minds in Christ Jesus. - **Philippians 4:6,7**

- Humble yourselves, therefore, under the mighty hand of God so that at the proper time he may exalt you, casting all your anxieties on him, because he cares for you. - **1 Peter 5:6,7**

- Commit your way to the LORD; trust in him, and he will act. - **Psalms 37:5**

- Cast your burden on the LORD, and he will sustain you; he will never permit the righteous to be moved. - **Psalms 55:22**

- Bless the LORD, O my soul, and all that is within me, bless his holy name! Bless the LORD, O my soul, and forget not all his benefits, who forgives all your iniquity, who heals all your diseases, who redeems your life from the pit, who crowns you with steadfast love and mercy, who satisfies you with good so that your youth is renewed like the eagle's. - **Psalms 103:1-5**

- Commit your work to the LORD, and your plans will be established. - **Proverbs 16:3**

- "Blessed is the man who trusts in the LORD, whose trust is the LORD. He is like a tree planted by water, that sends out its roots by the stream, and does not fear when heat comes, for its leaves remain green, and is not anxious in the year of drought, for it does not cease to bear fruit." - **Jeremiah 17:7,8**

- Do not be conformed to this world, but be transformed by the renewal of your mind, that by testing you may discern what is the will of God, what is good and acceptable and perfect. - **Romans 12:2**

- Count it all joy, my brothers, when you meet trials of various kinds, for you know that the testing of your faith produces steadfastness. And let steadfastness have its full effect, that you may be perfect and complete, lacking in nothing. - **James 1:2-4**
- "Come, everyone who thirsts, come to the waters; and he who has no money, come, buy and eat! Come, buy wine and milk without money and without price. Why do you spend your money for that which is not bread, and your labor for that which does not satisfy? Listen diligently to me, and eat what is good, and delight yourselves in rich food. Incline your ear, and come to me; hear, that your soul may live; and I will make with you an everlasting covenant, my steadfast, sure love for David. - **Isaiah 55:1-3**

- Though the fig tree should not blossom, nor fruit be on the vines, the produce of the olive fail and the fields yield no food, the flock be cut off from the fold and there be no herd in the stalls, yet I will rejoice in the LORD; I will take joy in the God of my salvation. GOD, the Lord, is my strength; he makes my feet like the deer's; he makes me tread on my high places. - **Habakkuk 3:17-19**

- Come to me, all who labor and are heavy laden, and I will give you rest. Take my yoke upon you, and learn from me, for I am gentle and lowly in heart, and you will find rest for your souls. For my yoke is easy, and my burden is light." - **Matthew 11:28-30**

- But the Lord answered her, "Martha, Martha, you are anxious and troubled about many things, but one thing is necessary. Mary has chosen the good portion, which will not be taken away from her." - **Luke 10:41-42**

Bible Verses To Read When You Feel Sad

- "When the righteous cry for help, the Lord hears and delivers them out of all their troubles. The Lord is near to the brokenhearted and saves the crushed in spirit. Many are the afflictions of the righteous, but the Lord delivers him out of them all. He keeps all his bones; not one of them is broken." - **Psalm 34:17-20**

- "Have I not commanded you? Be strong and courageous. Do not be frightened, and do not be dismayed, for the Lord your God is with you wherever you go." - **Joshua 1:9**

- "Come to me, all who labor and are heavy laden, and I will give you rest" - **Matt 11:28**

- "Rejoice always, pray without ceasing, give thanks in all circumstances; for this is the will of God in Christ Jesus for you." - **1 Thessalonians 5:16-18**

- "You keep him in perfect peace whose mind is stayed on you, because he trusts in you." - **Isaiah 26:3**

- "It is the Lord who goes before you. He will be with you; he will not leave you or forsake you. Do not fear or be dismayed." - **Deuteronomy 31:8**

- "And the peace of God, which surpasses all understanding, will guard your hearts and your minds in Christ Jesus." - **Philippians 4:7**

- "Peace I leave with you; my peace I give to you. Not as the world gives do I give to you. Let not your hearts be troubled, neither let them be afraid." - **John 14: 27**

Bible Verses To Help Overcome Resentment

- "Since, then, you have been raised with Christ, set your hearts on things above, where Christ is, seated at the right hand of God" - **Colossians 3:1**

- "We want each of you to show this same diligence to the very end, so that what you hope for may be fully realized" - **Hebrews 6:11**

- "Do not be overcome by evil, but overcome evil with good" - **Romans 12:21**

- "Are not five sparrows sold for two pennies? Yet not one of them is forgotten by God. Indeed, the very hairs of your head are all numbered. Don't be afraid; you are worth more than many sparrows" - **Luke 12:6-7**

- "You intended to harm me, but God intended it for good to accomplish what is now being done, the saving of many lives" - **Genesis 50:20**

- "Alexander the metalworker did me a great deal of harm. The Lord will repay him for what he has done" - **2 Timothy 4:14**

- "And when you stand praying, if you hold anything against anyone, forgive them, so that your Father in heaven may forgive you your sins" - **Mark 11:25**

- "Therefore, since we are receiving a kingdom that cannot be shaken, let us be thankful, and so worship God acceptably with reverence and awe, for our "God is a consuming fire" - **Hebrews 12:28-29**

Bible Verses About Making Mistakes

- "Against you, you only, have I sinned and done what is evil in your sight; so you are right in your verdict and justified when you judge" - **Psalm 51:4**

- "For I will forgive their wickedness and will remember their sins no more" - **Hebrews 8:12**

- "Forget the former things; do not dwell on the past" - **Isaiah 43:18**

- "But one thing I do: Forgetting what is behind and straining toward what is ahead, I press on toward the goal to win the prize for which God has called me heavenward in Christ Jesus" - **Philippians 3:13-14**

- "Create in me a pure heart, O God, and renew a steadfast spirit within me" - **Psalm 51:10**

- "For if you possess these qualities in increasing measure, they will keep you from being ineffective and unproductive in your knowledge of our Lord Jesus Christ. But whoever does not have them is nearsighted and blind, forgetting that they have been cleansed from their past sins" - **2 Peter 1:8-9**

- "Do not remember the sins of my youth and my rebellious ways; according to your love remember me, for you, Lord, are good" - Psalm 25:7

- "If we confess our sins, he is faithful and just and will forgive us our sins and purify us from all unrighteousness" - **1 John 1:9**

- "There is no difference between Jew and Gentile, for all have sinned and fall short of the glory of God" - **Romans 3:23**

- "Those whom I love I rebuke and discipline. So be earnest and repent" - **Revelation 3:19**

- "No temptation has overtaken you except what is common to mankind. And God is faithful; he will not let you be tempted beyond what you can bear. But when you are tempted, he will also provide a way out so that you can endure it" - **1 Corinthians 10:13**

- "But he said to me, 'My grace is sufficient for you, for my power is made perfect in weakness.' Therefore I will boast all the more gladly about my weaknesses, so that Christ's power may rest on me" - **2 Corinthians 12:9**

- "And we know that in all things God works for the good of those who love him, who have been called according to his purpose" - **Romans 8:28**

- "But I have prayed for you, Simon, that your faith may not fail. And when you have turned back, strengthen your brothers" - **Luke 22:32**

Bible verses about blessings

We often go to God with our requests, but have you considered going to God to thank him for your blessings? A journal of blessings is a great way to accentuate the blessings that you see in your life. Sure it is easy to ask for blessings, but it is just as easy to be thankful for blessings. Try it, get a journal or a notebook and start recording one blessing a day. Each new day brings a new blessing — no repeats allowed. Here are 20 good scripture quotes about blessings.

- For the sake of Christ, then, I am content with weaknesses, insults, hardships, persecutions, and calamities. For when I am weak, then I am strong. - 2 **Corinthians 12:10**

- For while we were still weak, at the right time Christ died for the ungodly. For one will scarcely die for a righteous person—though perhaps for a good person one would dare even to die—but God shows his love for us in that while we were still sinners, Christ died for us. - **Romans 5:6-8**

- Blessed is the man who remains steadfast under trial, for when he has stood the test he will receive the crown of life, which God has promised to those who love him. - **James 1:12**

- Henceforth there is laid up for me the crown of righteousness, which the Lord, the righteous judge, will award to me on that Day, and not only to me but also to all who have loved his appearing. - **2 Timothy 4:8**

- So I exhort the elders among you, as a fellow elder and a witness of the sufferings of Christ, as well as a partaker in the glory that is going to be revealed: shepherd the flock of God that is among you, exercising oversight, not under compulsion, but willingly, as God would have you; not for shameful gain, but eagerly; not domineering over those in your charge, but being examples to the flock. And when the chief Shepherd appears, you will receive the unfading crown of glory. - **1 Peter 5:1-4**

- For what is our hope or joy or crown of boasting before our Lord Jesus at his coming? Is it not you? For you are our glory and joy. - **1 Thessalonians 2:19-20**

- "If you will diligently listen to the voice of the LORD your God, and do that which is right in his eyes, and give ear to his commandments and keep all his statutes, I will put none of the diseases on you that I put on the Egyptians, for I am the LORD, your healer." **- Exodus 15:26**

- He will love you, bless you, and multiply you. He will also bless the fruit of your womb and the fruit of your ground, your grain and your wine and your oil, the increase of your herds and the young of your flock, in the land that he swore to your fathers to give you. **- Deuteronomy 7:13**

- "For if you truly amend your ways and your deeds, if you truly execute justice one with another, if you do not oppress the sojourner, the father-less, or the widow, or shed innocent blood in this place, and if you do not go after other gods to your own harm, then I will let you dwell in this place, in the land that I gave of old to your fathers forever..." **- Jeremiah 7:5-7**

- Thus says the LORD of hosts: If you will walk in my ways and keep my charge, then you shall rule my house and have charge of my courts, and I will give you the right of access among those who are standing here. Hear now, O Joshua the high priest, you and your friends who sit before you, for they are men who are a sign: behold, I will bring my servant the Branch. For behold, on the stone that I have set before Joshua, on a single stone with seven eyes, I will engrave its inscription, declares the LORD of hosts, and I will remove the iniquity of this land in a single day..." - **Zechariah 3:7-9**

- "...For if you keep silent at this time, relief and deliverance will rise for the Jews from another place, but you and your father's house will perish. And who knows whether you have not come to the kingdom for such a time as this?" - **Esther 4:14**

- Brother will deliver brother over to death, and the father his child, and children will rise against parents and have them put to death, and you will be hated by all for my name's sake. But the one who endures to the end will be saved. - **Matthew 10:21-22**

- Count it all joy, my brothers, when you meet trials of various kinds, for you know that the testing of your faith produces steadfastness. And let steadfastness have its full effect, that you may be perfect and complete, lacking in nothing. - **James 1:2**

- ..."Jesus, Master, have mercy on us." When he saw them he said to them, "Go and show yourselves to the priests." And as they went they were cleansed. (Jesus heals of leprosy) - **Luke 17:13**
- His brothers also came and fell down before him and said, "Behold, we are your servants." But Joseph said to them, "Do not fear, for am I in the place of God? As for you, you meant evil against me, but God meant it for good, to bring it about that many people should be kept alive, as they are today. - **Genesis 50:18-20**

- God answered Solomon, "Because this was in your heart, and you have not asked possessions, wealth, honor, or the life of those who hate you, and have not even asked long life, but have asked wisdom and knowledge for yourself that you may govern my people over whom I have made you king, and knowledge are granted to you. I will also give you riches, possessions, and honor, such as none of the kings had who were before you, and none after you shall have the like." - **2 Chronicles 1:11-12**

- When he was at table with them, he took the bread and blessed and broke it and gave it to them. And their eyes were opened, and they recognized him. And he vanished from their sight. They said to each other, "Did not our hearts burn within us while he talked to us on the road, while he opened to us the Scriptures?" And they rose that same hour and returned to Jerusalem. And they found the eleven and those who were with them gathered together, saying, "The Lord has risen indeed, and has appeared to Simon!" (after the Lord appeared to them on the road to Emmaus and they did not recognize the risen Lord) - **Luke 24:30-34**

- So Ananias departed and entered the house. And laying his hands on him he said, "Brother Saul, the Lord Jesus who appeared to you on the road by which you came has sent me so that you may regain your sight and be filled with the Holy Spirit." And immediately something like scales fell from his eyes, and he regained his sight. Then he rose and was baptized; and taking food, he was strengthened. (The conversion of Paul of Tarsus) - **Acts 9:17-19**

Bible Verses About Being Calm

- "When you pass through the waters, I will be with you; and through the rivers, they shall not overwhelm you; when you walk through fire you shall not be burned, and the flame shall not consume you." - **Isaiah 43:2**

- "For God gave us a spirit not of fear but of power and love and self-control." - **2 Timothy 1:7**

- "And he awoke and rebuked the wind and said to the sea, "Peace! Be still!" And the wind ceased, and there was a great calm." - **Mark 4:39**

- "I tell you, my friends, do not fear those who kill the body, and after that have nothing more that they can do. But I will warn you whom to fear: fear him who, after he has killed, has authority to cast into hell. Yes, I tell you, fear him**!"- Luke 12:4-5**

- "He made the storm be still and the waves of the sea were hushed. Then they were glad that the waters were quiet, and he brought them to their desired haven." - **Psalm 107:29-30**

- "Be angry and do not sin; do not let the sun go down on your anger, and give no opportunity to the devil." - **Ephesians 4:26-27**

- "Let not your hearts be troubled. Believe in God; believe also in me." - **John 14:1**

- "Let not your hearts be troubled. Believe in God; believe also in me" - **John 14:1**

- "If the anger of the ruler rises against you, do not leave your place for calmness will lay great offenses to rest." - **Ecclesiastes 10:4**

Bible Verses to Pray Over Your Child

Our children can know about our relationship with Jesus without ever having ownership of this knowledge for themselves. We must pray and be sensitive to the leading of the Spirit to guide them to know Jesus for themselves. When given the right promptings, they will eventually learn to recognize His voice speaking to their hearts.

- "The Lord bless you and keep you; the Lord make his face shine on you and be gracious to you; the Lord turn his face toward you and give you peace" - **Numbers 6:24-26**

- "In the same way, let your light shine before others, that they may see your good deeds and glorify your Father in heaven" - **Matthew 5:16**

- "For the Spirit God gave us does not make us timid, but gives us power, love and self-discipline" - **2 Timothy 1:7**

- "Do not be anxious about anything, but in every situation, by prayer and petition, with thanksgiving, present your requests to God" - **Philippians 4:6**

- "Be strong and courageous. Do not be afraid or terrified because of them, for the Lord your God goes with you; he will never leave you nor forsake you" - **Deuteronomy 31:6**

- "But grow in the grace and knowledge of our Lord and Savior Jesus Christ. To him be glory both now and forever! Amen" - **2 Peter 3:18**

- "Stand firm then, with the belt of truth buckled around your waist, with the breastplate of righteousness in place" - **Ephesians 6:14**

- "I want to know Christ—yes, to know the power of his resurrection and participation in his sufferings, becoming like him in his death, and so, somehow, attaining to the resurrection from the dead" - **Philippians 3:10-11**

Bible Verses for Grief and Grieving

- Surely he has borne our griefs and carried our sorrows; yet we esteemed him stricken, smitten by God, and afflicted. 5But he was pierced for our transgressions; he was crushed for our iniquities; upon him was the chastisement that brought us peace, and with his wounds we are healed. 6All we like sheep have gone astray; we have turned—every one—to his own way; and the Lord has laid on him the iniquity of us all. - **Isaiah 53:4-6**

- Then Jacob tore his garments and put sackcloth on his loins and mourned for his son many days. 35 All his sons and all his daughters rose up to comfort him, but he refused to be comforted and said, "No, I shall go down to Sheol to my son, mourning." Thus his father wept for him. - **Genesis 37:34-35**

- And the people of Israel wept for Moses in the plains of Moab thirty days. Then the days of weeping and mourning for Moses were ended. - **Deuteronomy 34:8**

- David therefore sought God on behalf of the child. And David fasted and went in and lay all night on the ground. 17 And the elders of his house stood beside him, to raise him from the ground, but he would not, nor did he eat food with them. - **2 Samuel 12:16-17**

- The heart of the wise is in the house of mourning, but the heart of fools is in the house of mirth. - **Ecclesiastes 7:4**

- For everything there is a season, and a time for every matter under heaven: 2 a time to be born, and a time to die; a time to plant, and a time to pluck up what is planted; 3 a time to kill, and a time to heal; a time to break down, and a time to build up; 4 a time to weep, and a time to laugh; a time to mourn, and a time to dance - **Ecclesiastes 3:1-4**

- In the day of my trouble I seek the Lord; in the night my hand is stretched out without wearying; my soul refuses to be comforted. - **Psalms 77:2**

- If your law had not been my delight, I would have perished in my affliction. - **Psalms 119:92**

- Fear not, for I am with you; be not dismayed, for I am your God; I will strengthen you, I will help you, I will uphold you with my righteous right hand. - **Isaiah 41:10**

- Brothers, I do not consider that I have made it my own. But one thing I do: forgetting what lies behind and straining forward to what lies ahead, 14 I press on toward the goal for the prize of the upward call of God in Christ Jesus. - **Philippians 3:13-14**

- Submit yourselves therefore to God. Resist the devil, and he will flee from you. - **James 4:7**

- Precious in the sight of the Lord is the death of his saints. - **Psalms 116:15**

- This is my comfort in my affliction, that your promise gives me life. - **Psalms 119:50**

- And the ransomed of the Lord shall return and come to Zion with singing; everlasting joy shall be upon their heads; they shall obtain gladness and joy, and sorrow and sighing shall flee away. - **Isaiah 51:11**

- For I consider that the sufferings of this present time are not worth comparing with the glory that is to be revealed to us. - **Romans 8:18**

- When the perishable puts on the imperishable, and the mortal puts on immortality, then shall come to pass the saying that is written: "Death is swallowed up in victory." "O death, where is your victory? O death, where is your sting?" - **1 Corinthians 15:54-55**

- But we do not want you to be uninformed, brothers, about those who are asleep, that you may not grieve as others do who have no hope. - **1 Thessalonians 4:13**

- And I heard a voice from heaven saying, "Write this: Blessed are the dead who die in the Lord from now on." "Blessed indeed," says the Spirit, "that they may rest from their labors, for their deeds follow them!" - **Revelation 14:13**

- He will wipe away every tear from their eyes, and death shall be no more, neither shall there be mourning, nor crying, nor pain anymore, for the former things have passed away." - **Revelation 21:4**

Bible Verses About Confidence

- For not in my bow do I trust, nor can my sword save me. - **Psalms 44:6**

- For the LORD will be your confidence and will keep your foot from being caught. - **Proverbs 3:26**

- A scoffer seeks wisdom in vain, but knowledge is easy for a man of understanding. - **Proverbs 14:6**

- I have confidence in the Lord that you will take no other view, and the one who is troubling you will bear the penalty, whoever he is. - **Galatians 5:10**

- And I am sure of this, that he who began a good work in you will bring it to completion at the day of Jesus Christ. - **Philippians 1:6**

- For we are the circumcision, who worship by the Spirit of God and glory in Christ Jesus and put no confidence in the flesh. - **Philippians 3:3**

- I can do all things through him who strengthens me. - **Philippians 4:13**

- Let us then with confidence draw near to the throne of grace, that we may receive mercy and find grace to help in time of need. - **Hebrews 4:16**

- So we can confidently say, "The Lord is my helper; I will not fear; what can man do to me?" - **Hebrews 13:6**

- And this is the confidence that we have toward him, that if we ask anything according to his will he hears us. - **1 John 5:14**

- Be strong and courageous. Do not fear or be in dread of them, for it is the LORD your God who goes with you. He will not leave you or forsake you." - **Deuteronomy 31:6**

- I will not be afraid of many thousands of people who have set themselves against me all around. - **Psalms 3:6**

- Trust in the LORD with all your heart, and do not lean on your own understanding. In all your ways acknowledge him, and he will make straight your paths. - **Proverbs 3:5**

- Only be strong and very courageous, being careful to do according to all the law that Moses my servant commanded you. Do not turn from it to the right hand or to the left, that you may have good success wherever you go. - **Joshua 1:7**

- Have I not commanded you? Be strong and courageous. Do not be frightened, and do not be dismayed, for the LORD your God is with you wherever you go." - **Joshua 1:9**

- But they who wait for the LORD shall renew their strength; they shall mount up with wings like eagles; they shall run and not be weary; they shall walk and not faint. - **Isaiah 40:31**

- Fear not, for I am with you; be not dismayed, for I am your God; I will strengthen you, I will help you, I will uphold you with my righteous right hand. - **Isaiah 41:10**

- Now when they saw the boldness of Peter and John, and perceived that they were uneducated, common men, they were astonished. And they recognized that they had been with Jesus. - **Acts 4:13**

- Therefore, my beloved brothers, be steadfast, immovable, always abounding in the work of the Lord, knowing that in the Lord your labor is not in vain. - **1 Corinthians 15:58**

- And he set combat commanders over the people and gathered them together to him in the square at the gate of the city and spoke encouragingly to them, saying, "Be strong and courageous. Do not be afraid or dismayed before the king of Assyria and all the horde that is with him, for there are more with us than with him. - **2 Chronicles 32:6-7**

- "Therefore do not be anxious about tomorrow, for tomorrow will be anxious for itself. Sufficient for the day is its own trouble. - **Matthew 6:34**

Bible Verses About Being Grateful

It's a gift from God for us to be grateful because it's impossible to be discontented and thankful at the same time. There are so many people in the world today who enjoy His sunshine or rain, His provision of food, clothing, and shelter—and they never stop to thank Him. Let the people of God sing His praises in the morning, afternoon, and evening. May we never grow tired of being grateful!

- "Give thanks to the Lord, for he is good; his love endures forever" **- 1 Chronicles 16:34**

- "Give thanks in all circumstances; for this is God's will for you in Christ Jesus" **- 1 Thessalonians 5:18**

- "And whatever you do, whether in word or deed, do it all in the name of the Lord Jesus, giving thanks to God the Father through him" **- Colossians 3:17**

- "Thanks be to God for his indescribable gift!" **- 2 Corinthians 9:15**

- "Thanks be to God, who delivers me through Jesus Christ our Lord!" **- Romans 7:25**

- "I will give thanks to you, Lord, with all my heart; I will tell of all your wonderful deeds" **- Psalms 9:1**

- "Do not be anxious about anything, but in every situation, by prayer and petition, with thanksgiving, present your requests to God" **- Philippians 4:6**

Bible Verses for Hard Times

- Before I was afflicted I went astray, but now I keep your word. You are good and do good; teach me your statutes - **Psalms 119:67-68**

- I cried aloud to the LORD, and he answered me from his holy hill. - **Psalms 3:4**

- When the righteous cry for help, the LORD hears and delivers them out of all their troubles. - **Psalm 34:17**

- ...call upon me in the day of trouble; I will deliver you, and you shall glorify me. - **Psalms 50:15**

- Trust in the LORD with all your heart, and do not lean on your own understanding. In all your ways acknowledge him, and he will make straight your paths. - **Proverbs 3:5-6**

- Seek the LORD while he may be found; call upon him while he is near - **Isaiah 55:6**

- Why are you cast down, O my soul, and why are you in turmoil within me? Hope in God; for I shall again praise him, my salvation - **Psalms 42:5**

- I cried to him with my mouth, and high praise was on my tongue. If I had cherished iniquity in my heart, the Lord would not have listened. But truly God has listened; he has attended to the voice of my prayer. Blessed be God, because he has not rejected my prayer or removed his steadfast love from me! - **Psalms 66:17-20**

- Blessed is he whose help is the God of Jacob, whose hope is in the LORD his God, who made heaven and earth, the sea, and all that is in them, who keeps faith forever - **Psalms 146:5-6**

- About midnight Paul and Silas were praying and singing hymns to God, and the prisoners were listening to them - **Acts 16:25**

- Now to him who is able to do far more abundantly than all that we ask or think, according to the power at work within us, to him be glory in the church and in Christ Jesus throughout all generations, forever and ever. Amen. - **Ephesians 3:20-21**

- And God is able to make all grace abound to you, so that having all sufficiency in all things at all times, you may abound in every good work. - **2 Corinthians 9:8**

- He delivered us from such a deadly peril, and he will deliver us. On him we have set our hope that he will deliver us again. - **2 Corinthians 1:10**

- He has delivered us from the domain of darkness and transferred us to the kingdom of his beloved Son - **Colossians 1:13**

- We have this as a sure and steadfast anchor of the soul, a hope that enters into the inner place behind the curtain, where Jesus has gone as a forerunner on our behalf, having become a high priest forever after the order of Melchizedek. - **Hebrews 6:19-20**

- Blessed is the man who remains steadfast under trial, for when he has stood the test he will receive the crown of life, which God has promised to those who love him. - **James 1:12**

- Count it all joy, my brothers, when you meet trials of various kinds, for you know that the testing of your faith produces steadfastness. And let steadfastness have its full effect, that you may be perfect and complete, lacking in nothing. - **James 1:2-4**

- It is good for me that I was afflicted, that I might learn your statutes. The law of your mouth is better to me than thousands of gold and silver pieces. - **Psalms 119:71-72**

- I know, O LORD, that your rules are righteous, and that in faithfulness you have afflicted me. Let your steadfast love comfort me according to your promise to your servant. - **Psalms 119:75-76**

- Through him we have also obtained access by faith into this grace in which we stand, and we rejoice in hope of the glory of God. Not only that, but we rejoice in our sufferings, knowing that suffering produces endurance, and endurance produces character, and character produces hope, and hope does not put us to shame, because God's love has been poured into our hearts through the Holy Spirit who has been given to us. - **Romans 5:2-5**

- And we know that for those who love God all things work together for good, for those who are called according to his purpose. - **Romans 8:28**

Bible Verses About Guidance

- **2 Timothy 3:16-17** All Scripture is breathed out by God and profitable for teaching, for reproof, for correction, and for training in righteousness, 17 that the man of God may be complete, equipped for every good work. - **2 Timothy 3:16-17**

- "... Is anything too hard for the Lord? At the appointed time I will return to you, about this time next year, and Sarah shall have a son." - **Genesis 18:14**

- Then I proclaimed a fast there, at the river Ahava, that we might humble ourselves before our God, to seek from him a safe journey for ourselves, our children, and all our goods. So we fasted and implored our God for this, and he listened to our entreaty. - **Ezra 8:21, 23 21**

- Lead me in your truth and teach me, for you are the God of my salvation; for you I wait all the day long. - **Psalms 25:5**

- I will instruct you and teach you in the way you should go; I will counsel you with my eye upon you. - **Psalms 32:8**

- The steps of a man are established by the Lord, when he delights in his way; though he fall, he shall not be cast headlong, for the Lord upholds his hand. - **Psalms 37:23-24**

- Trust in the Lord with all your heart, and do not lean on your own understanding.6 In all your ways acknowledge him, and he will make straight your paths. - **Proverbs 3:5-6**

- But the Lord said to me, "Do not say, 'I am only a youth'; for to all to whom I send you, you shall go, and whatever I command you, you shall speak. Do not be afraid of them, for I am with you to deliver you, declares the Lord." - **Jeremiah 1:7-8**

- "Ask, and it will be given to you; seek, and you will find; knock, and it will be opened to you ..." - **Matthew 7:7**

- If any of you lacks wisdom, let him ask God, who gives generously to all without reproach, and it will be given him. 6 But let him ask in faith, with no doubting, for the one who doubts is like a wave of the sea that is driven and tossed by the wind. 7 For that person must not suppose that he will receive anything from the Lord; he is a double-minded man, unstable in all his ways. - **James 1:5-8**

- And Samuel said to all the house of Israel, "If you are returning to the Lord with all your heart, then put away the foreign gods and the Ashtaroth from among you and direct your heart to the Lord and serve him only, and he will deliver you out of the hand of the Philistines." - **1 Samuel 7:3**

- So Saul died for his breach of faith. He broke faith with the Lord in that he did not keep the command of the Lord, and also consulted a medium, seeking guidance. 14 He did not seek guidance from the Lord. Therefore the Lord put him to death and turned the kingdom over to David the son of Jesse. - **1 Chronicles 10:13-14**

- Where there is no guidance, a people falls, but in an abundance of counselors there is safety. - **Proverbs 11:14**

- There is a way that seems right to a man, but its end is the way to death. - **Proverbs 14:12**

- For a people shall dwell in Zion, in Jerusalem; you shall weep no more. He will surely be gracious to you at the sound of your cry. As soon as he hears it, he answers you. 20 And though the Lord give you the bread of adversity and the water of affliction, yet your Teacher will not hide himself anymore, but your eyes shall see your Teacher. And your ears shall hear a word behind you, saying, "This is the way, walk in it," when you turn to the right or when you turn to the left. 22 Then you will defile your carved idols overlaid with silver and your gold-plated metal images. You will scatter them as unclean things. You will say to them, "Be gone!" - **Isaiah 30:19-22**

- Beloved, do not believe every spirit, but test the spirits to see whether they are from God, for many false prophets have gone out into the world. - **1 John 4:1**

- For the foolishness of God is wiser than men, and the weakness of God is stronger than men. - **1 Corinthians 1:25**

- And the Spirit of the Lord shall rest upon him, the Spirit of wisdom and understanding, the Spirit of counsel and might, the Spirit of knowledge and the fear of the Lord. - **Isaiah 11:2**

- But the Helper, the Holy Spirit, whom the Father will send in my name, he will teach you all things and bring to your remembrance all that I have said to you. - **John 14:26**

- Likewise the Spirit helps us in our weakness. For we do not know what to pray for as we ought, but the Spirit himself intercedes for us with groanings too deep for words. - **Romans 8:26**

Bible Verses To Help Overcome Insecurity

- "Do not be anxious about anything, but in everything by prayer and supplication with thanksgiving let your requests be made known to God. And the peace of God, which surpasses all understanding, will guard your hearts and your minds in Christ Jesus." - **Philippians 4:6-7**

- "Therefore, since we have been justified by faith, we have peace with God through our Lord Jesus Christ. Through him we have also obtained access by faith into this grace in which we stand, and we rejoice in hope of the glory of God." - **Romans 5:1-2**

- "There is no fear in love, but perfect love casts out fear. For fear has to do with punishment, and whoever fears has not been perfected in love." - **First John 4:18**

- "Therefore I tell you, do not be anxious about your life, what you will eat or what you will drink, nor about your body, what you will put on. Is not life more than food, and the body more than clothing?" - **Matthew 6:25**

- "No temptation has overtaken you that is not common to man. God is faithful, and he will not let you be tempted beyond your ability, but with the temptation he will also provide the way of escape, that you may be able to endure it." - **First Corinthians 10:13**

- "There is therefore now no condemnation for those who are in Christ Jesus. For the law of the Spirit of life has set you free in Christ Jesus from the law of sin and death." - **Romans 8:1-2**

- "Peace I leave with you; my peace I give to you. Not as the world gives do I give to you. Let not your hearts be troubled, neither let them be afraid." - **John 14:27**

Bible Verses About Letting Go

- "Let all bitterness and wrath and anger and clamor and slander be put away from you, along with all malice. Be kind to one another, tenderhearted, forgiving one another, as God in Christ forgave you." - **Ephesians 4:31-32**

- "Brothers, I do not consider that I have made it my own. But one thing I do: forgetting what lies behind and straining forward to what lies ahead, I press on toward the goal for the prize of the upward call of God in Christ Jesus." - **Philippians 3:13-14**

- "Remember not the former things, nor consider the things of old. Behold, I am doing a new thing; now it springs forth, do you not perceive it? I will make a way in the wilderness and rivers in the desert." - **Isaiah 43:18-19**

- "Do you not know that in a race all the runners run, but only one receives the prize? So run that you may obtain it." - **First Corinthians 9:24**

- "And we know that for those who love God all things work together for good, for those who are called according to his purpose." - **Romans 8:28**

- "Casting all your anxieties on him, because he cares for you." - **First Peter 5:7**

- "Do not be anxious about anything, but in everything by prayer and supplication with thanksgiving let your requests be made known to God." - **Philippians 4:6**

- "Whoever conceals his transgressions will not prosper, but he who confesses and forsakes them will obtain mercy." - **Proverbs 28:13**

- "Therefore, since we are surrounded by so great a cloud of witnesses, let us also lay aside every weight, and sin which clings so closely, and let us run with endurance the race that is set before us, looking to Jesus, the founder and perfecter of our faith, who for the joy that was set before him endured the cross, despising the shame, and is seated at the right hand of the throne of God." - **Hebrews 12:1-2**

- "Be angry and do not sin; do not let the sun go down on your anger, and give no opportunity to the devil." - **Ephesians 4:26-27**

Bible Verses About Patience

- The LORD is slow to anger and great in power, and the LORD will by no means clear the guilty. His way is in whirlwind and storm, and the clouds are the dust of his feet. - **Nahum 1:3**

- Do you suppose, O man—you who judge those who practice such things and yet do them yourself—that you will escape the judgment of God? Or do you presume on the riches of his kindness and forbearance and patience, not knowing that God's kindness is meant to lead you to repentance? - **Romans 2:3-4**

- The Lord is not slow to fulfill his promise as some count slowness, but is patient toward you, not wishing that any should perish, but that all should reach repentance. - **2 Peter 3:9**

- Then the LORD said, "My Spirit shall not abide in man forever, for he is flesh: his days shall be 120 years." - **Genesis 6:3**

- He who is often reproved, yet stiffens his neck, will suddenly be broken beyond healing. - **Proverbs 29:1**

- Because the sentence against an evil deed is not executed speedily, the heart of the children of man is fully set to do evil. - **Ecclesiastes 8:11**

- The LORD could no longer bear your evil deeds and the abominations that you committed. Therefore your land has become a desolation and a waste and a curse, without inhabitant, as it is this day. - **Jeremiah 44:22**

- "Then he will say to those on his left, 'Depart from me, you cursed, into the eternal fire prepared for the devil and his angels...'" (Jesus speaking) - **Matthew 25:41**

- The signs of a true apostle were performed among you with utmost patience, with signs and wonders and mighty works. - **2 Corinthians 12:12**

- But the fruit of the Spirit is love, joy, peace, patience, kindness, goodness, faithfulness, gentleness, self-control; against such things there is no law. - **Galatians 5:22-23**

- I therefore, a prisoner for the Lord, urge you to walk in a manner worthy of the calling to which you have been called, with all humility and gentleness, with patience, bearing with one another in love, eager to maintain the unity of the Spirit in the bond of peace. - **Ephesians 4:1-3**

- May you be strengthened with all power, according to his glorious might, for all endurance and patience with joy, giving thanks to the Father, who has qualified you to share in the inheritance of the saints in light. - **Colossians 1:11-12**

- Put on then, as God's chosen ones, holy and beloved, compassionate hearts, kindness, humility, meekness, and patience, bearing with one another and, if one has a complaint against another, forgiving each other; as the Lord has forgiven you, so you also must forgive. - **Colossians 3:12-13**

- "... As for that in the good soil, they are those who, hearing the word, hold it fast in an honest and good heart, and bear fruit with patience." (Jesus speaking in the parable of the sower) - **Luke 8:15**

- He will render to each one according to his works: to those who by patience in well-doing seek for glory and honor and immortality, he will give eternal life... - **Romans 2:6-7**

- For in this hope we were saved. Now hope that is seen is not hope. For who hopes for what he sees? But if we hope for what we do not see, we wait for it with patience. - **Romans 8:24-25**

- But I received mercy for this reason, that in me, as the foremost, Jesus Christ might display his perfect patience as an example to those who were to believe in him for eternal life. - **1 Timothy 1:16**

- And we desire each one of you to show the same earnestness to have the full assurance of hope until the end, so that you may not be sluggish, but imitators of those who through faith and patience inherit the promises. - **Hebrews 6:11-12**

Bible Verses About Purpose

- But you are a chosen people, a royal priesthood, a holy nation, God's special possession, that you may declare the praises of him who called you out of darkness into his wonderful light. - **1 Peter 2:9**

- This man was handed over to you by God's deliberate plan and foreknowledge; and you, with the help of wicked men, put him to death by nailing him to the cross. - **Acts 2:23**

- "Now when David had served God's purpose in his own generation, he fell asleep; he was buried with his ancestors and his body decayed. - **Acts 13:36**

- For in him all things were created: things in heaven and on earth, visible and invisible, whether thrones or powers or rulers or authorities; all things have been created through him and for him. - **Colossians 1:16**

- There is a time for everything, and a season for every activity under the heavens: - **Ecclesiastes 3:1**

- For I know the plans I have for you," declares the LORD, "plans to prosper you and not to harm you, plans to give you hope and a future. - **Jeremiah 29:11**

- Great are your purposes and mighty are your deeds. Your eyes are open to the ways of all mankind; you reward each person according to their conduct and as their deeds deserve. - **Jeremiah 32:19**

- "I know that you can do all things; no purpose of yours can be thwarted. - **Job 42:2**

- But the Pharisees and the experts in the law rejected God's purpose for themselves, because they had not been baptized by John.) - **Luke 7:30**

- The LORD works out everything to its proper end— even the wicked for a day of disaster. - **Proverbs 16:4**

- Many are the plans in a person's heart, but it is the LORD's purpose that prevails. - **Proverbs 19:21**

- The purposes of a person's heart are deep waters, but one who has insight draws them out. - **Proverbs 20:5**

- But the plans of the LORD stand firm forever, the purposes of his heart through all generations. - **Psalm 33:11**

- The LORD will vindicate me; your love, LORD, endures forever— do not abandon the works of your hands. - **Psalm 138:8**

- And we know that in all things God works for the good of those who love him, who have been called according to his purpose. - **Romans 8:28**

- For we are God's handiwork, created in Christ Jesus to do good works, which God prepared in advance for us to do. - **Ephesians 2:10**

- I make known the end from the beginning, from ancient times, what is still to come. I say, 'My purpose will stand, and I will do all that I please.' - **Isaiah 46:10**

- I make known the end from the beginning, from ancient times, what is still to come. I say, 'My purpose will stand, and I will do all that I please.' 11 From the east I summon a bird of prey; from a far-off land, a man to fulfill my purpose. What I have said, that I will bring about; what I have planned, that I will do. - **Isaiah 46:10-11**

- Now all has been heard; here is the conclusion of the matter: Fear God and keep his commandments, for this is the duty of all mankind. 14 For God will bring every deed into judgment, including every hidden thing, whether it is good or evil. - **Ecclesiastes 12:13-14**

- Then Jesus came to them and said, "All authority in heaven and on earth has been given to me. 19 Therefore go and make disciples of all nations, baptizing them in the name of the Father and of the Son and of the Holy Spirit, 20 and teaching them to obey everything I have commanded you. And surely I am with you always, to the very end of the age." - **Matthew 28:18-20**

Forgiveness Bible Verses

Read passages that offer biblical guidance on forgiveness and how important it is to forgive others as we have been forgiven by the blood of Christ. With the grace and mercy shown to us, we are always able to start new with God. When we repent, we are given full forgiveness of our sins because of the death and resurrection of Jesus.

In light of our new beginning, God commands that in return, we forgive others and extend grace as we have been shown grace. It can be one of the hardest things we face in life! The pain and hurt others cause us is real and great. But, the pain of living with bitterness and unforgiveness can poison your soul and destroy you. When we forgive others, we are not saying what they did was OK, but we are releasing them to God and letting go of its hold on us.

- Bear with each other and forgive one another if any of you has a grievance against someone. Forgive as the Lord forgave you. - **Colossians 3:13**

- For if you forgive other people when they sin against you, your heavenly Father will also forgive you. 15 But if you do not forgive others their sins, your Father will not forgive your sins. - **Matthew 6:14-15**

- So watch yourselves. "If your brother or sister sins against you, rebuke them; and if they repent, forgive them. 4 Even if they sin against you seven times in a day and seven times come back to you saying 'I repent,' you must forgive them." - **Luke 17:3-4**

- Get rid of all bitterness, rage and anger, brawling and slander, along with every form of malice. 32 Be kind and compassionate to one another, forgiving each other, just as in Christ God forgave you. - **Ephesians 4:31-32**

- If we confess our sins, he is faithful and just and will forgive us our sins and purify us from all unrighteousness. - **1 John 1:9**

- "I, even I, am he who blots out your transgressions, for my own sake, and remembers your sins no more. 26 Review the past for me, let us argue the matter together; state the case for your innocence. - **Isaiah 43:25-26**

- Repent, then, and turn to God, so that your sins may be wiped out, that times of refreshing may come from the Lord - **Acts 3:19**

- "Come now, let us settle the matter," says the LORD. "Though your sins are like scarlet, they shall be as white as snow; though they are red as crimson, they shall be like wool. - **Isaiah 1:18**

- Therefore, if anyone is in Christ, the new creation has come: The old has gone, the new is here! - **2 Corinthians 5:17**

- In him we have redemption through his blood, the forgiveness of sins, in accordance with the riches of God's grace - **Ephesians 1:7**

- Then he adds: "Their sins and lawless acts I will remember no more." - **Hebrews 10:17**

- The Lord our God is merciful and forgiving, even though we have rebelled against him - **Daniel 9:9**

- For he has rescued us from the dominion of darkness and brought us into the kingdom of the Son he loves, 14 in whom we have redemption, the forgiveness of sins. - **Colossians 1:13-14**

- As far as the east is from the west, so far has he removed our transgressions from us. - **Psalm 103:12**

- In accordance with your great love, forgive the sin of these people, just as you have pardoned them from the time they left Egypt until now." 20 The LORD replied, "I have forgiven them, as you asked. 21 Nevertheless, as surely as I live and as surely as the glory of the LORD fills the whole earth - **Numbers 14:19-21**

- Who is a God like you, who pardons sin and forgives the transgression of the remnant of his inheritance? You do not stay angry forever but delight to show mercy. 19 You will again have compassion on us; you will tread our sins underfoot and hurl all our iniquities into the depths of the sea. - **Micah 7:18-19**

- "This, then, is how you should pray: " 'Our Father in heaven, hallowed be your name, 10 your kingdom come, your will be done, on earth as it is in heaven. 11 Give us today our daily bread. 12 And forgive us our debts, as we also have forgiven our debtors. 13 And lead us not into temptation, but deliver us from the evil one.' 14 For if you forgive other people when they sin against you, your heavenly Father will also forgive you. 15 But if you do not forgive others their sins, your Father will not forgive your sins. - **Matthew 6:9-15**
- And when you stand praying, if you hold anything against anyone, forgive them, so that your Father in heaven may forgive you your sins." - **Mark 11:25**

- This is my blood of the covenant, which is poured out for many for the forgiveness of sins. - **Matthew 26:28**

The Promises of God

- And because of his glory and excellence, he has given us great and precious promises. These are the promises that enable you to share his divine nature and escape the world's corruption caused by human desires. - **2 Peter 1:4**

- For I know the plans I have for you," says the Lord. "They are plans for good and not for disaster, to give you a future and a hope. - **Jeremiah 29:11**

- "Come to me, all you who are weary and burdened, and I will give you rest. Take my yoke upon you and learn from me, for I am gentle and humble in heart, and you will find rest for your souls. - **Matthew 11:28-29**

- He gives power to the weak, and strength to the powerless. Even youths will become weak and tired, and young men will fall in exhaustion. But those who trust in the Lord will find new strength. They will soar high on wings like eagles. They will run and not grow weary. They will walk and not faint. - **Isaiah 40:29-31**

- And this same God who takes care of me will supply all your needs from his glorious riches, which have been given to us in Christ Jesus. - **Philippians 4:19**

- But all who listen to me will live in peace, untroubled by fear of harm." - **Proverbs 1:33**

- No, despite all these things, overwhelming victory is ours through Christ, who loved us. And I am convinced that nothing can ever separate us from God's love. Neither death nor life, neither angels nor demons, neither our fears for today nor our worries about tomorrow—not even the powers of hell can separate us from God's love. No power in the sky above or in the earth below— indeed, nothing in all creation will ever be able to separate us from the love of God that is revealed in Christ Jesus our Lord. - **Romans 8:37-39**

- "I am leaving you with a gift—peace of mind and heart. And the peace I give is a gift the world cannot give. So don't be troubled or afraid. - **John 14:27**

- If you confess with your mouth that Jesus is Lord and believe in your heart that God raised him from the dead, you will be saved. - **Romans 10:9**

- For the wages of sin is death, but the free gift of God is eternal life through Christ Jesus our Lord. - **Romans 6:23**

Conclusion

We often believe that no one else could possibly know what we are going through, but God always knows because He is the omniscient and omnipresent God. "Trust in the LORD with all your heart and lean not on your own understanding; in all your ways submit to him, and he will make your paths straight" (Proverbs 3:5-6). This means if we are committed to and trust in God with a faithful heart, He will help us through the struggles and obstacles in our paths.

When you are overwhelmed with health problems, bad news, or relationship struggles, the Word of God can be your source of supernatural help. Don't give up! God promises greater things in store - a future filled with promise and hope!

Made in the USA
Las Vegas, NV
28 March 2023